SUGAR ART
Ideas

RICE PAPER
FLOWERS

SUGAR ART
Ideas

RICE PAPER FLOWERS

MARGARET HYDE

Consultant: NICHOLAS LODGE
Series Editor: ALISON LEACH

SELECT
EDITIONS

I would like to dedicate this book to my husband Ron for his love and support, and to
my sons Stephen and Edward, and my mum. A very special thanks to my friend and
assistant Audrey, and my Personnel Manager Rennie for her help and support. My
thanks to Winnie, Janet and Jane, my family and all my friends, and colleagues in both
bakery and teaching careers, not forgetting my pupils for their interest,
encouragement and support over the past several years.

Published 1992 by The Promotional Reprint Co Ltd,
Exclusively for Selecta Book Ltd,
Devizes UK and the Book Company,
Sydney in Australia

Printed and bound in Hong Kong through Bookbuilders Ltd

—ACKNOWLEDGEMENTS—

The publishers would like to thank Winnie Bassett of 'Winnie B', 61 Waverley
Crescent, Plumstead, London SE18 for her help in supplying equipment used in this
book.

Warning
Cocktail sticks and wired flowers must only be used for display purposes in sugarcraft. Great care
should always be taken to ensure there is no possibility of any particles being eaten accidentally.

CONTENTS

FOREWORD

Flowers – from those growing wild in the hedgerows to the most exotic blooms – are a continual source of wonder and delight. They have been used since time immemorial to express our emotions; artists and skilled craftsmen have reproduced them in many different materials through the ages . . . and now Margaret Hyde has developed a new technique using rice paper, which is both easily obtainable and inexpensive.

Margaret is an experienced sugarcraft tutor and has taught this subject in London for several years. I congratulate her on extending her skills to the making of rice paper flowers.

I know that the beautiful photographs, clearly defined step-by-step instructions and the use of templates, together with the ideas for using the flowers on many occasions, will immediately capture your imagination.

As a dedicated sugarcraft enthusiast, I am sure that this book will stimulate everyone with a love of craftwork and will inspire beginners to take that first step towards creating 'a thing of beauty'. The sense of personal achievement in mastering a simple flower makes one eager to try the more complicated species also to be found in this delightful book.

I wish the author great success and every reader much enjoyment in practising this fascinating new craft.

Eileen Swann

INTRODUCTION

Rice paper has been available for many years and has been mainly used in industry to form machine-moulded roses, and it appeared no one had realized its full decorative potential.

Although rice paper has recently been used for modelling purposes, I decided to try making some light fragile flowers and to discover how to develop certain petal shapes. I started with a water-lily and then experimented with more complicated flowers such as dahlias and chrysanthemums, which would be almost impossible to make if using paste. Rice paper is so light that many more petals can be added. Centres are not used in the making of rice paper flowers. I have included some examples of how to use rice paper flowers instead of fragile paste

flowers on cakes. When slightly moistened with water, rice paper sticks to itself and the flowers can be used immediately. Rice paper flowers are inexpensive to make and have the obvious advantage of being almost unbreakable which simplifies the transportation of finished arrangements.

This book explains how to colour, cut and shape petals to form many varieties of flowers and how to wire them for special uses. Every flower is illustrated with step-by-step photographs.

When you have practised making the various flowers shown in this book, you may find other ways of using them both in your creative sugarcraft and for social events such as dinner parties.

Margaret Hyde

EQUIPMENT

rice paper
blossom tint dusting powder colours
icing (confectioner's) sugar
paintbrushes
tweezers
fabric-covered floristry wires
ribbons
floristry tape
baskets for arrangements
posy frills

Choosing rice paper

Rice paper may vary slightly in
thickness according to the
supplier, but there is no
preference for any particular
kind. It must be stored flat in a
dry place because it sticks to
itself when moistened and it
will crack or break if folded in
half.

Selecting brushes and colours

Soft paintbrushes such as sable
hair are recommended for
making the flowers, the finer
ones being used to moisten the
outer edges of petals and the
thicker ones to moisten larger
pieces of rice paper, such as
those used for making leaves.
   Only dry colours may be
used on rice paper. The
blossom tint dusting colours
are available in a wide range of
colours. If you add a small
amount of icing sugar to some
blossom tint dusting colour, it
goes further and improves the
even blending of the colour on
the rice paper. Do not use
liquid colours as they would
affect the rice paper, causing it
to shrink and be wrinkled
when dry.

BASIC TECHNIQUES

Colouring rice paper

The smooth side is the right side and the bevelled side is the wrong side of rice paper. Colouring must be done on the right side of the paper. Add a little icing sugar to some blossom tint dusting colour and blend with your fingers. Put some of the blended powder on to the right side of the rice paper and rub it in gently, following the grain of the paper. Shake off the excess colour.

Making a cone

Cut a rectangle of rice paper about 5 × 2.5-cm (2 × 1-in). Turn the paper so that the wrong side is facing uppermost. Fold the top right-hand corner of the paper under and pull it over the left-hand side of the oblong, curling it under. Hold it in position and moisten with a damp paintbrush to secure the seam. Trim off the excess paper at the base so that the cone can stand up steadily.

Shaping a lily petal

This method may be used for the Chrysanthemum, Decorative Dahlia and Snowdrop petals (*see pages 20, 26 and 44*).

Cut the basic petal shape and cut from the base up the centre to slightly below halfway. Moisten one side of the cut section and overlap the opposite section, pressing into position to form a curve. These petals may be used in reverse, according to the type of flower being produced.

For an open flower, cut and overlap the petal on the coloured side of the paper. For a closed flower, cut and overlap the petal on the wrong side of the petal and turn the petal over so that the colour is shown.

Curling petals

Cut and shape petals as required and roll each one gently round the end of a paintbrush to curl it. The curl may be made on the wrong side to produce an incurving petal. For an open flower, the curl must be made on the right side of the petal.

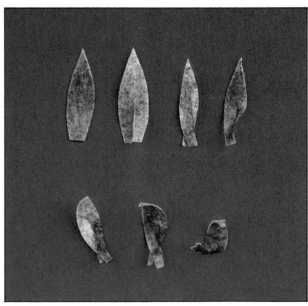

Making leaves and stems

Using green-coloured rice paper, cut squares or rectangles as appropriate and moisten the wrong side of the paper with the coloured side facing downwards. Place a second piece of paper on top with the coloured side facing upwards. Press to secure. Cut out the leaf shape as required.

To make stems for use on cakes or flat arrangements, follow the procedure above and cut thin strips from rice paper rectangles to the required length. When these dry, the stems will curl slightly. Any unused pieces of paper may be kept for future use but they will become quite firm and wrinkled when dry.

Attaching wires to flat flowers

This method is ideal for flowers such as Christmas Roses, Daffodils and Daisies (*see pages 18, 22 and 24*). The flowers must be dry before attaching the wires.

1 Cut a medium-size wire to the required length. Wrap a very small piece of moistened rice paper around the top of the wire and form a small loop as shown. Bend the loop sideways to form a hook. Moisten the hook and press gently but firmly to the base of the flower to secure. Leave to dry.

2 Place the calyx leaves over the wire and the base of the flower as this will both camouflage the hook and hold the wire firmly in position.

Wiring flowers together

CORSAGE Begin with the leaf or ribbon tail and wire in all the chosen main flowers. Complete the corsage with some gypsophila and ribbon loops.

STRAIGHT SPRAY This is a very popular arrangement. Begin with the flower buds and gradually add the smaller flowers, increasing the size of the spray. Gradually wire in the larger flowers with foliage and ribbon loops.

Ribbon loops

1 Cut thin strips of appropriately coloured rice paper. Moisten one end of a strip and fold over, gently pressing to secure. Continue in this way making as many loops as required. Moisten the base of one loop and attach a second loop to it, pressing to secure. Attach a third loop.

If curled ribbons are required, roll a strip of coloured rice paper gently around the base of a paintbrush and unwind carefully. Moisten one end and press to the base of ribbon loops. Continue until all the loops and ribbons are made.

Bows

1 Cut two strips about 12-mm ($\frac{1}{2}$-in) wide in appropriately coloured rice paper for the loops. Cut a third strip of the same width but slightly shorter for the centre band. Cut two further strips for the ribbon tails.

2 Fold one of the strips by moistening one end and pressing to secure against the other end. Fold the second strip in the same way. Moisten the end of one half of the bow and attach the other half, overlapping slightly. Press to secure. Fold the centre band into three and wrap it round the centre of the bow, as shown. Moisten the ends and seal the seam.

3 Slightly moisten the ribbon tails and join together, as shown. Moisten the centre back of the bow and attach it to the ribbon tails. Press to secure.

CACTUS DAHLIA

1 Make a rice paper cone (*see page 10*). Make templates from the patterns and cut out small, medium and large petals in yellow-coloured rice paper. Moisten the centre of each petal and crease lengthways.

2 Moisten the base of the small petals and attach them to the cone upright with the folds facing outwards. Continue until the top of the cone is covered. Moisten the base of the medium petals and place slightly below the small petals with the folds now uppermost as shown.

3 When enough medium petals are on the cone, moisten the base of the larger petals and place between the other petals, gradually moving slightly down the cone until a full-blown flower is created. Leave to dry and then cut away the excess cone.
  Cut small thin green-coloured rice paper petals and attach in position underneath the dahlia to form a calyx, covering the hole at the base of the flower.

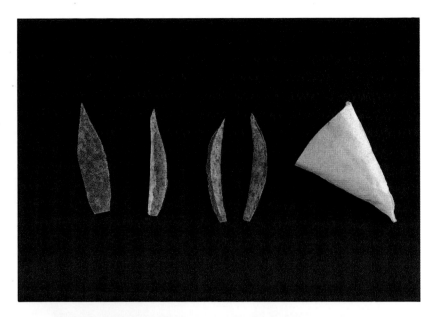

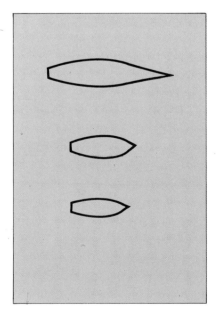

CARNATION

1 Make a template from the
pattern and cut five circles
of yellow-coloured rice paper.
Cut a fluted edge to each
circle. Make the stamens by
cutting a narrow, 2.5-cm (1-in)
long strip of rice paper, the
same colour as the petals and
then cut this strip in half
lengthways. Make several short
cuts with scissors on each
curve of the fluted edge of
each circle and longer cuts
between each curve.

2 Working on the first petal,
moisten half the petal to
just below the fluted edge and
fold it in half. Moisten half of
the folded petal to just below
the fluted edge and fold once
more. Lay the two stamens in
the centre and squeeze the base
of the petal tightly.
    Cut the remaining petals in
half. Moisten one to just below
the fluted edge and place it
outside the first petal, turning
gently to secure the edges in
position. Moisten another and
attach it in the same way,
squeezing gently at the base of
the flower. Continue to attach
petal halves around the flower
until they are all in position.

3 Make a template from the
pattern and cut three petals
in green-coloured rice paper.
Moisten each petal and place
them, slightly overlapping each
other, around the base of the
carnation to form a calyx.

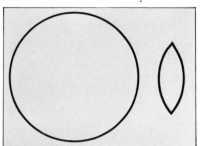

Miniature roses and carnations

This arrangement of miniature
roses and carnations are taped
together with leaves and
gypsophila to form a dainty
straight spray.

CHRISTMAS ROSE

1 Cut oblongs of white rice paper. Make a template from the pattern and cut petal shapes as shown. Five petals are required for each flower. Gently brush green colour on to the tip of the base of each petal. Moisten the base of the first petal and attach the second petal, slightly overlapping the first and pressing gently to secure. Moisten the base of the third petal and attach it, slightly overlapping the second petal. Continue in this way until all five petals are equally spaced and the flower is complete.

2 Cut a narrow strip of yellow-coloured rice paper about 2.5-cm × 12-mm (1 × ½-in) and cut a fine fringe. Moisten the base and gently roll the fringe up, squeezing the base firmly. Cut off the excess. Moisten the base and attach it to the centre of the Christmas rose.

Using a very fine brush, touch the centre of the yellow cluster with a tiny amount of red colour. With a slightly damp, clean brush, gently brush fine lines from the outside edge of the petals towards the centre. This will give the petals a waxed appearance.

3 To make the leaves, cut squares of green-coloured rice paper and join together as described on page 11. Make templates from the patterns and cut out four of the large size and three of the small size. Using a damp brush, moisten the first small leaf and place the second leaf in position, slightly overlapping. Moisten the third small leaf and place in the centre of the two joined leaves. Then moisten a large leaf and attach it behind the three small leaves. Moisten and add the remaining three large leaves behind the smaller leaves.

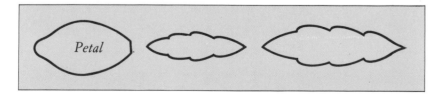

Petal

CHRYSANTHEMUM

The chrysanthemum flowers and leaves are arranged in a small white egg cup-shaped pastillage vase. Dry florist's foam is used in this container to hold the arrangement in position, but a ball of pastillage may be used instead.

1 About 50–60 petals are required for each flower. Make a rice paper cone (*see page 10*). Make a template from the larger pattern and cut out the petals in suitably coloured rice paper. Shape the petals as for a water-lily (*see page 48*). Roll the curved petals gently round the handle of a medium-sized paintbrush to emphasize the curves.

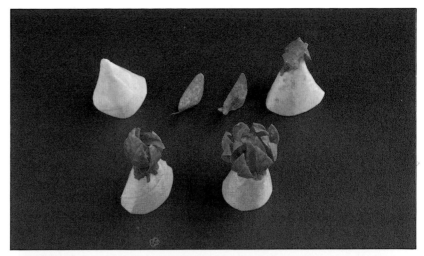

Moisten the base of the first petal and attach it just below the top of the rice paper cone. Attach the second petal, slightly overlapping the first. Work around the cone until the tip cannot be seen. Continue to add more petals, overlapping the edges of the previous layers and pressing firmly to the cone, keeping the height of the petals in each layer almost level. When completing the last two layers, push each petal slightly backwards to obtain an opening effect.

Using a damp paintbrush, moisten the inside of the cone at the base of the flower and squeeze the cone tightly to close the flower and force the petals to open further. When dry, use scissors to cut away the excess cone.

2 Make a template from the smaller pattern and cut out eight petal shapes in green-coloured rice paper. Moisten the base of each petal and attach, slightly overlapping, to the base of the flower.

3 To make the leaves, cut oblongs of green-coloured rice paper and join as described on page 11. Make a template from the pattern and cut out the leaves. Allow to dry. The leaves may be graduated in size, if liked.

DAFFODIL

1 Make a template from the
pattern and cut out six
petals in yellow-coloured rice
paper. Moisten the base of
three petals and arrange them
in ten, two and six o'clock
positions, as shown, gently
pressing them into position to
meet at the centre. Moisten the
bases of the remaining three
petals and attach them between
the first three petals and
meeting in the centre. Press to
secure.

2 Make a small cone (*see page
10*) 2.5-cm × 12-mm (1 ×
½-in) from a strip of yellow-
coloured rice paper. Fold the
cone flat and cut a fluted frill
across the widest part as
shown. Moisten the base of the
cone and ease it into position
in the centre of the daffodil.
Gently moisten the fluted edge
of the trumpet and ease it
outwards to obtain a curved
effect.
   Cut a narrow strip of
yellow-coloured rice paper and
make a fringe along one edge.
Moisten below the fringe and
roll up tightly to form a
stamen cluster. Moisten the
base and place in the centre of
the trumpet.

3 To make the leaves cut
oblongs of green-coloured
rice paper and join as described
on page 11. Make a template
from the pattern and cut out
the leaf. Allow to dry. If the
leaf is to be wired, insert a fine
wire between the two oblongs
of paper when joining them.

Daffodils with rice paper stems

The daffodils are attached to
rice paper stems to form a
delicate spray for use on a
cake.

DAISY

1 Make a template from the larger pattern and cut out about twelve petals for each flower in white rice paper. Moisten along the centre of each petal and gently crease lengthways. Moisten the base of the first petal and attach the second petal, slightly overlapping the first at an angle, as shown. Moisten the third petal at the base and attach it to the second petal, overlapping it slightly at an angle. Continue to add petals until a full circle is formed.

A second layer of petals may be added by moistening the base of the first petal of the second layer and securing it between two petals of the first layer. Continue to overlap petals until a full circle is formed.

2 Make a stamen cluster for the centre by cutting a narrow strip of yellow-coloured rice paper and cutting a fine fringe. Moisten the base of the fringe with a damp paintbrush and roll the strip, gently squeezing it to form a posy. Cut away the excess base of the posy, moisten with a damp paintbrush and place it in the centre of the flower, pressing firmly to secure.

Make a template from the smaller pattern and cut out petal shapes in green-coloured rice paper. Attach to the underside of the daisy, overlapping each one so as to cover the centre completely.

25

DECORATIVE DAHLIA

1 Make a cone (*see page 10*).
  Make templates of the three
sizes of petal from the patterns
and cut out in suitably
coloured rice paper. Moisten
the edges of the small and
medium petals and shape as
shown, curling them inwards.
Moisten the edges of the large
petals and shape as shown,
curling them outwards.
Moisten the bases of the small
petals and place each one
curling inwards and
overlapping the next around
the tip of the cone. Continue
until all the small petals are
attached.
  Moisten the bases of the
medium petals and attach them
behind and overlapping the
edges of the small petals.
Continue to add petals,
overlapping the previous layers
until all are attached. Moisten
the bases of the largest petals
and place in position behind
the medium petals, continuing
to work around the flower
until it is complete.

2 When dry, remove the
  excess cone and attach small
petal shapes in green-coloured
rice paper to form a calyx
around the hole in the base of
the flower.

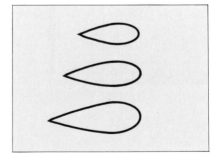

FREESIA

1 This flower may be made directly on to wire. Make a template from the pattern and cut out six petals in mauve-coloured rice paper. Moisten the base of the first petal and attach the second petal slightly overlapping, as shown. Moisten the base of the third petal and attach to the second petal, slightly overlapping as before.

2 Cut a small strip of yellow-coloured rice paper about 12 mm (½-in) in length and cut a fringe with scissors. Moisten the base of the fringe and wrap it around the flower wire.

  Moisten the bases of all three petals and wrap around the base of the stamen cluster. Squeeze gently at the base to secure. Moisten the base of the fourth petal and attach it to the outside of the flower, between the first and second petals. Add the fifth and sixth petals overlapping the other petals, securing at the base.

3 Cut out two small petal shapes in green-coloured rice paper. Moisten the first petal and place it near the base of the flower, overlapping the wire and wrap firmly around the wire. Add the second petal opposite the first and wrap around the wire to secure.

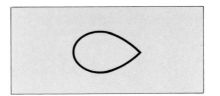

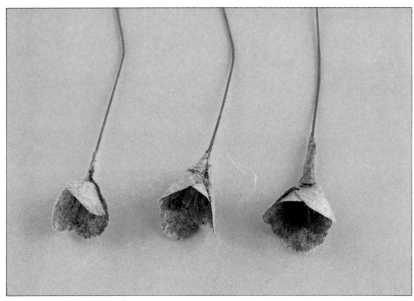

MARGUERITE

1 Make a template from the pattern and cut out about fourteen petals in white rice paper. Moisten the base of one petal and press a second petal into position, slightly overlapping the first, as shown. Moisten the base of a third petal and press into position, overlapping the second. Continue in this way until a full circle is formed.

2 Cut a narrow strip in yellow-coloured rice paper and cut a fine fringe along one edge. Moisten the base, gently roll the fringe and squeeze it tightly. Cut off the excess from the base with scissors. Moisten the base and press it firmly into position in the centre of the flower.

Make a template from the pattern and cut out several small petal shapes in green-coloured rice paper. Moisten the base of each petal and attach to the underside of the flower in the centre, as shown, to form a calyx.

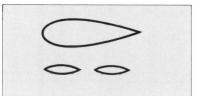

NARCISSUS

1 Make a template from the larger pattern and cut out six petals in yellow-coloured rice paper. Moisten the base of three petals and arrange them in ten, two and six o'clock positions, as shown. Moisten the remaining three petals and attach them between the first three petals and meeting in the centre. Press to secure.

2 Make a template from the smaller pattern and cut out six rounded petals in orange-coloured rice paper. Moisten the base of the first petal and attach the second, slightly overlapping the first, as shown. Moisten the third petal and attach it to the second petal, slightly overlapping. Moisten the lower edge of the third petal and wrap it round to secure it to the first petal to form a loose trumpet. Press firmly together at the base.

Moisten the last three petals and secure each to the outside edges of the others. Lightly moisten the top edges of the petals and curl them slightly outwards. Moisten the base of the trumpet and press it firmly on to the centre of the flower.

Cut a very narrow strip about 12-mm ($\frac{1}{2}$-in) long in yellow-coloured rice paper. Carefully cut a fringe with small scissors. Moisten the base of the fringe, roll it up gently and squeeze together to form a stamen cluster. Moisten the base and place it in the trumpet with tweezers.

3 To make the leaf, cut oblongs of green-coloured rice paper and join as described on page 11. Make a template from the pattern for a daffodil leaf (*see page 22*) and cut out in the same way.

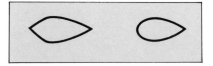

Daffodil and narcissi

This arrangement makes an attractive gift or a seasonable table decoration for Easter. A little basket complements these small daffodils and narcissi, interspersed with leaves. A ball of sugarpaste may be used instead of florist's foam.

PANSY

1 Make templates from the
patterns and cut out four
'A'-shaped and one 'B'-shaped
petals. Moisten the top edges
of the four 'A'-shaped petals,
easing them gently to become
fluted. Leave to dry for a few
minutes. Moisten the edges of
the 'B'-shaped petal and leave
to dry.

2 Moisten the base of one
petal and position it,
overlapping the base of the
second, as shown. Moisten the
base of the third petal and
attach it to the base of the first
petal, as shown. Moisten the
base of the fourth petal and
position it below the second
petal and slightly overlapping
the third petal at centre.

3 Moisten the centre of the
'B'-shaped petal and attach
it below the third and fourth
petals in the centre. When dry,
mark fine dark lines with a
nearly dry paintbrush from the
centre of the 'B'-shaped petal,
using a tiny amount of petal
dust powder mixed to a thick
paste.

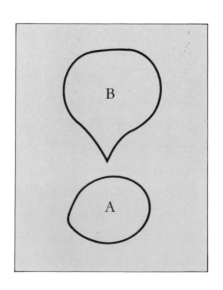

PRIMROSE

1 Cut a piece of green-coloured rice paper measuring 5 × 2.5-cm (2 × 1-in) and make a cone (*see page 10*). Make a template from the pattern and cut out five petals in pale yellow-coloured rice paper. Moisten the base of the first petal and place it just below the tip of the cone. Moisten the base of the second petal and place it slightly overlapping the first. Continue until all five petals are in position, overlapping each other.

2 Using scissors, make four cuts along the length of the cone. Slightly moisten the inside of the cone and overlap the cut sections to form a long slim calyx, as shown.
   Moisten a small amount of yellow blossom tint with a wet paintbrush and mix to a paste. Remove any excess paste from the paintbrush with a tissue. Paint a small star in the centre of each primrose, as shown.
   Using scissors, remove any part of green cone that may be protruding at the centre of the flower.

3 To make the leaf, cut out several pieces of light green-coloured rice paper, about 5 × 3.5-cm (2 × 1¼-in). Join together as described on page 11. Make a template from the pattern and cut out the leaf shape, fluting the edge slightly. Use a damp paintbrush to mix a little yellow/green blossom tint to a paste. Paint on the leaf to give a two-tone effect. The leaf will become crinkled as it dries.

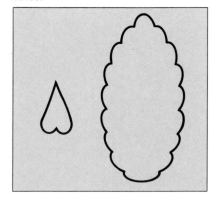

ROSE

1 Make a cone (*see page 10*). Make templates from the patterns and cut out four of each size of petal in pink-coloured rice paper. Moisten the first small petal all over with a damp paintbrush and wrap it tightly around the top of the cone, as shown. Moisten the second petal to just below the top edge and attach it behind the join of the first petal. Wrap around gently and secure the lower edges, using a damp paintbrush. Moisten the third petal and place it overlapping the second petal, as shown. Moisten the fourth petal and overlap as previously described.

2 Moisten the lower halves of the two medium petals and place them on opposite sides of the bud, overlapping a little at the back. Gently moisten the outside edge of each petal and bend the edges back slightly to obtain a curved effect. Moisten the base of the third medium petal, place it at the back of the rose and shape slightly, using a damp paintbrush. Moisten the fourth petal and place it at the front of the rose. Moisten the edges to shape, as shown.

3 Moisten the undersides of the remaining four large petals and shape each one. Allow to dry for a few minutes. Moisten the base of the first shaped petal, placing it to the left side of the rose. Moisten the base of the second petal, placing it to the back and overlapping the inside of the first petal. Moisten the third and fourth petals and place them in position, overlapping as before and completing the flower, as shown. When dry, trim off the excess cone.

Make a template from the pattern and cut out five slim leaves in green-coloured rice paper. Moisten each and attach them evenly across the base hole, as shown, to form the calyx.

To make the leaves, cut out squares of green-coloured rice paper and join together as described on page 11. Make a template from the pattern and cut out the required number of leaf shapes in green-coloured rice paper. Snip out small sections to give the leaves spiked edges. Moisten the edges where·necessary and gently bend to shape to create a natural effect. If toning is required on outer areas of the leaves, tint with petal dust colours.

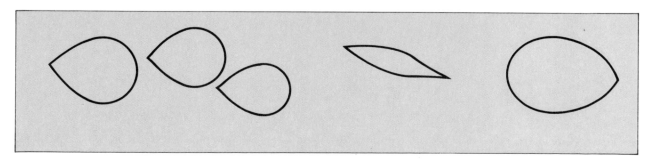

Red roses

Red roses, gypsophila and rose
leaves are taped together to
form an attractive straight
spray which is finished with
red ribbons.

Roses, carnations and gypsophila

The wired roses, carnations and gypsophila are arranged in a yellow boat-shaped vase made of pastillage. Yellow petal dust has been rubbed into the container to give an uneven appearance, making it look old and mellow.

SNOWDROP

1 These flowers must be made on wire. Begin by cutting a thin piece of green-coloured rice paper, moistening it and wrapping it tightly around the wire to form a bud.

Make a template from the pattern and cut out three small petals in white rice paper. Moisten the base of the first petal and attach the second, slightly overlapping it. Moisten and place the third petal in position. Slightly moisten the bases of these three petals and wrap them around the wire, as shown.

2 Make a template from the pattern and cut out three long slim petals and shape them as for the water-lily (*see page 48*). Slightly curl them round the paintbrush. Moisten the base of each petal and attach them, overlapping the edges of the petals on the wire, as shown.

3 Using a moistened paintbrush, paint a touch of green petal dust on to the outside of the small petals. Moisten and wrap a tiny strip of green-coloured rice paper around the base of the flower.

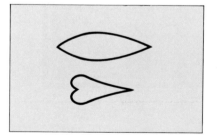

Snowdrops

Snowdrops with leaves and green ribbon are arranged in this tall straight pastillage container which has been rubbed with green petal dust to give an antique appearance.

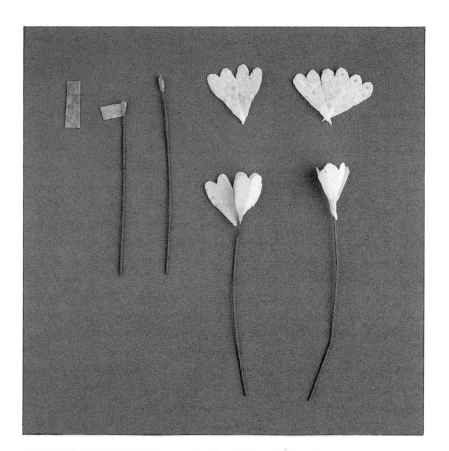

SWEET PEA

1 Attach a small piece of rice
  paper to a wire as shown
and leave to dry. Make
templates from the patterns of
the three petals, and cut out in
pink-coloured rice paper.
Moisten one half of the 'A'-
shaped petal and place the wire
in the centre. Press the two
halves together to form a bud.

2 Cut out two 'B'-shaped
  petals. Moisten the edge of
one side of one petal and
attach it to the underside of the
bud and gently press into
position. Attach the second
petal on the opposite side of
the bud and secure in position.
Moisten the outside edges of
the petals to give a frilled
effect.
   Cut one 'C'-shaped petal.
Moisten along the centre of the
petal and pinch both sides
together. Moisten the base of
the flower and attach the large
petal to it. Ease into shape,
curling it slightly downwards.

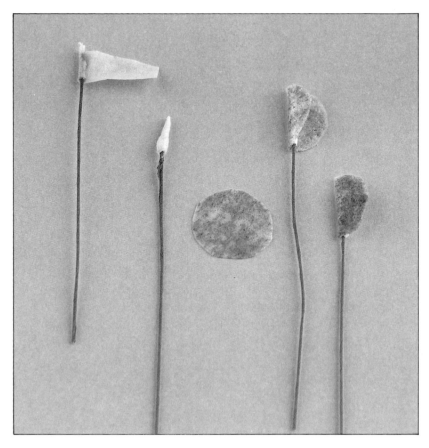

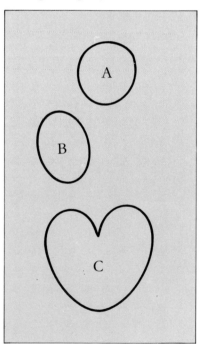

WATER-LILY

1 Make templates from the patterns and cut out the different petal shapes in white rice paper. About twelve large petals are required for the outer layer, ten medium for the second layer and eight small for the inner layer. Shape the petals as described on page 10. Moisten one side of the first large petal near the base and place the second petal on it, slightly overlapping as shown. Press it into position. Continue in this way until all the large petals are in position.

To make the second layer, moisten the base of a medium petal and place it between two petals of the first layer. Continue in this manner with the remaining petals, overlapping as before. When assembling the inner layer of small petals, place them in a more upright position and allow them to dry.

2 To form a stamen cluster, cut a narrow strip of yellow-coloured rice paper and cut a very fine fringe along one edge. Moisten the base of the fringe and roll the strip closely but gently to form a posy. Squeeze the base tightly to secure and, using scissors, cut the excess part away. Moisten the cut base with a damp paintbrush and place in the centre of the lily, pressing firmly to secure.

To make the leaf, cut 3-cm (1¼-in) squares of green-coloured rice paper. Join together as described on page 10. Make a template from the pattern and cut out the leaf shape. Allow to dry.

GYPSOPHILA

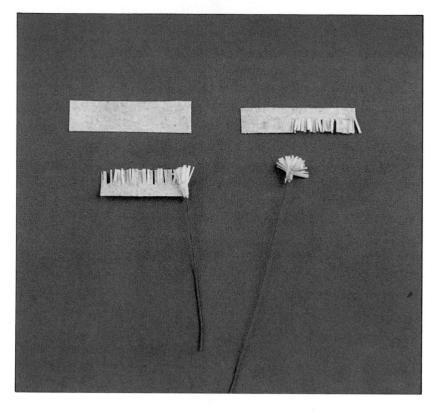

1 Cut a narrow strip of white rice paper and cut a fine fringe along one edge. Moisten the other edge and attach it to a fine wire, gently winding it around to form a small flower. Squeeze the base of the flower to secure and allow the fringe to fan out. When dry, gently trim the top of the flower with scissors to obtain a flat top.

MAIDENHAIR FERN

1 Cut small squares of green-coloured rice paper and join together as described on page 11. Make a template from the pattern and cut maidenhair shapes to form one section of the fern. Continue in this manner until enough sections are made. Tape each section to a main wire to form a spray as shown (*see page 12*).

Pink roses

Pink roses, leaves and
gypsophila complement each
other in this arrangement.
They are taped together to
form a traditional straight
spray and finished with pink
ribbon.

CHRISTMAS CAKE

Christmas cake

The Christmas roses, leaves, holly and fir cones on the royal-iced Christmas cake are not wired. They are attached to the cake with royal icing and arranged in a crescent shape to complement the plain shell border and matching green ribbon on the side of the cake. This design is ideal for any beginner.

Christmas table arrangement

This arrangement will complement any table at Christmas time. It consists of wired Christmas roses, holly and fir cones inserted into a ball of sugarpaste or a piece of dry florist's foam, placed in an oval-shaped basket or similar container.

Candlestick wreath

This arrangement consists of wired Christmas roses, holly, fir cones and ribbon, joined together to form a wreath. A candlestick with a non-drip candle can be placed in the centre making an attractive table decoration to complement a matching floral arrangement.

Christmas napkin rings

These are made from wired Christmas roses, fir cones and holly, arranged in a small group and taped to the napkin rings.

Place name settings

The place name settings are made from sugar pastillage, cut to the required shape, with a holly pattern border and decorated with Christmas roses and holly.

Christmas tree decorations

Another idea for using rice paper flowers for Christmas is to tape wired Christmas roses, holly and fir cones with ribbons to create decorations to hang on a Christmas tree, or on a wall.

FIR CONES

1 Make a small cone (*see page 10*). Make templates from the patterns and cut out a large number of the smaller shapes in brown-coloured rice-paper. With the coloured side face-down, curve each petal as described on page 10. Moisten the base of the first shape and place it so it covers part of the tip of the cone. Moisten another shape and place it slightly overlapping the first. Continue to add shapes until the tip of the cone is covered.

2 Moisten and attach a second layer of shapes, placing them between the edges of the previous ones and securing them further down the cone. Continue to add shapes, gently easing out the last to give an opened look. When dry cut off the excess part of the cone (if appropriate) and place a few of the larger shapes across the open base.

HOLLY LEAVES AND BERRIES

1 Cut squares of green-coloured rice paper about 5 × 3-cm (2 × 1¼-in) and join together as described on page 11. Make a template from the pattern and cut as many holly shapes as required. Moisten along the centre and edges of each leaf and bend to shape as required.

Cut small strips of red-coloured rice paper, about 5-cm × 12-mm (2 ×½-in). Moisten each strip and roll it up gently to form a holly berry. Leave to dry. Re-tint with red colouring if necessary.

FINE FERN

1 Cut two large squares of green-coloured rice paper and join together as described on page 11. Cut numerous, long, thin leaf shapes from the squares and some small leaves.

2 Moisten the base of a small leaf and place at the top of a fine wire, gently squeezing the moistened part around the wire. Moisten the base of a second leaf shape and place it in position as shown, wrapping the moistened part around the wire. Continue to add leaves until the required size of the fern is achieved. Leave to dry.

Holly Leaves

Fir cones

DAHLIAS, MARGUERITES AND FERN

This floral arrangement consists
of wired decorative and cactus
dahlias, marguerites and fern.
The vase is made of coloured
pastillage and rubbed with petal
dust to give a terracotta
appearance. Small plastic or
glass vases would also be
suitable for this floral
arrangement if there were no
time to make the container.

DAISY POSY

Wire stems are attached to
these daisies and then the
flowers are arranged in this
unusual posy holder with white
and yellow ribbons to
complement them. The wire
stems are taped together neatly
for easier handling.

ORCHID CELEBRATION CAKE

Three wired orchids with ribbon and gypsophila are taped and placed on the sugar fondant-covered special occasion cake. Matching ribbon on the side of the cake adds the finishing touch. The orchids are examples of the more complicated flowers that can be made once the basic techniques are mastered.

GOLDEN WEDDING ROSE CAKE

Unwired roses and leaves are attached to the sugar fondant-covered cake with royal icing and arranged in a spray. The matching ribbon on the side of the cake picks up the colour of the roses.

SWEET BOXES

Matching ribbons and roses complement these small gift boxes, which could contain special chocolates.

WATER-LILY

This large water-lily may be
used as a table decoration and
filled with sugared almonds.